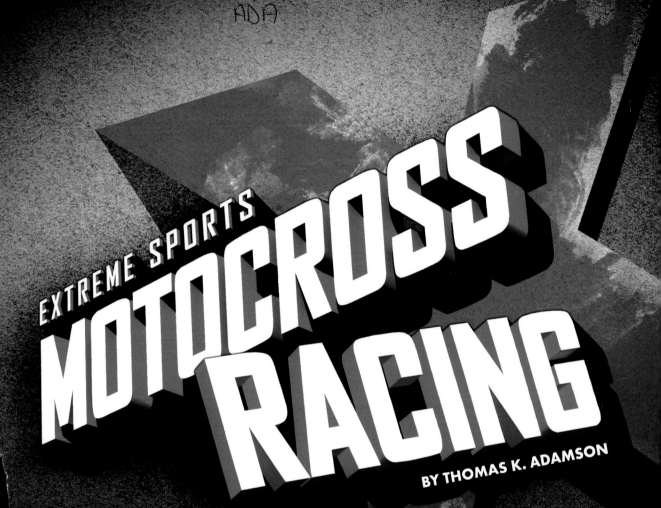

EXTREME SPORTS

MOTOCROSS
RACING

BY THOMAS K. ADAMSON

EPIC

BELLWETHER MEDIA • MINNEAPOLIS, MN

EPIC BOOKS are no ordinary books. They burst with intense action, high-speed heroics, and shadows of the unknown. Are you ready for an Epic adventure?

T 106924

This edition first published in 2016 by Bellwether Media, Inc.

No part of this publication may be reproduced in whole or in part without written permission of the publisher. For information regarding permission, write to Bellwether Media, Inc., Attention: Permissions Department, 5357 Penn Avenue South, Minneapolis, MN 55419.

Library of Congress Cataloging-in-Publication Data

Adamson, Thomas K., 1970-
  Motocross Racing / by Thomas K. Adamson.
     pages cm. – (Epic: Extreme Sports)
  Summary: "Engaging images accompany information about motocross racing. The combination of high-interest subject matter and light text is intended for students in grades 2 through 7"– Provided by publisher.
  Audience: Ages 7 to 12
  Includes bibliographical references and index.
  ISBN 978-1-62617-276-0 (hardcover: alk. paper)
  1. Motocross–Juvenile literature. 2. Extreme sports–Juvenile literature. 3. ESPN X-Games–Juvenile literature. I. Title.
  GV1060.12.A38 2016
  796.7'56–dc23

                    2015013361

Printed in the United States of America, North Mankato, MN.

TABLE OF CONTENTS

Endurocross Win! 4

Motocross Racing 8

Motocross History 12

Motocross Gear 16

The Competition 18

Glossary 22

To Learn More..................... 23

Index................................. 24

WARNING
The riders in this book are
professionals. Always wear
a helmet and other safety gear
when you are on a motorcycle.

ENDUROCROSS WIN!

Taddy Blazusiak speeds around the first corner. He cruises into the second place position early in the Endurocross race at the 2014 X Games. He launches off the first big jump. He passes the leader!

Blazusiak works his bike around a corner filled with rocks. The rider in second place tries to pass. **Lapped** riders get in his way! Blazusiak pulls away to win X Games gold.

X GAMES CHANGES

The X Games has held different types of motocross races over the years. Its first Endurocross event was in 2011.

7

MOTOCROSS RACING

In motocross racing, motorcycle riders zoom around **challenging** dirt tracks. Many motocross races are held outside. Supercross races are packed in stadiums.

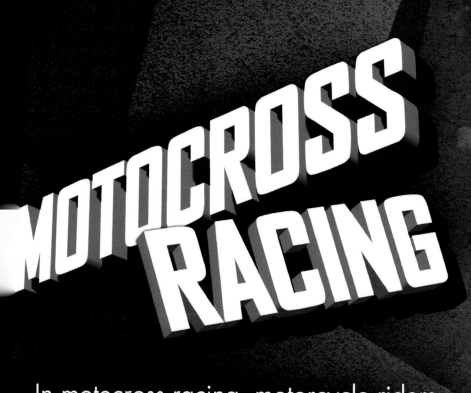

ON TRACK

Motocross tracks have tight corners and big jumps. Many have a set of small bumps called whoops.

Some motocross races offer other challenges. Enduro events are long races held on rough trails. Endurocross races have many **obstacles** and are held in stadiums. Hillclimbs are races up **steep** hills.

A ROUGH RIDE
Endurocross riders race over logs and rocks. There are even piles of chopped wood!

MOTOCROSS RACING TERMS

enduro—a long motocross race that tests a rider's strength and endurance

endurocross—a long motocross race with many obstacles that is held in a stadium

hillclimb—a motocross race that tests which rider goes the farthest up a steep hill

motos—motocross races

scrambles—races in the early days of motorcycle racing

supercross—a motocross race that takes place in a stadium

trials—races held on rough trails in the early days of motorcycle racing

whoops—a series of bumps close together on a motocross track

hillclimb

MOTOCROSS HISTORY

Motorcycle racing grew popular in Europe in the early 1900s. Riders raced on trails and bicycle tracks. Over time, jumps were added to the races. The new sport became known as motocross.

WANT TO RACE?
Early motorcycle
races were called
trials and scrambles.

In the 1960s, motocross racing came to the United States. Fans were amazed by the riders' speed and skills. Soon, Americans began winning big races. The sport's popularity continues to grow!

THE FIRST SUPERCROSS

In 1972, the first American motocross championship race was held in a stadium in Los Angeles, California. It was called the Superbowl of Motocross.

MOTOCROSS GEAR

Motocross is a dangerous sport. Every racer wears a helmet and goggles. A chest and back protector covers the shoulders and body. A long-sleeved **jersey** and pants protect the arms and legs.

NICE KICKS

Some motocross boots have steel toes to protect the riders' feet.

THE COMPETITION

Motocross races are called motos. Riders are **organized** into different **classes** based on the size of their engine. Racers compete in two motos per event.

EVENT SCORING

Riders earn points based on where they finish in each moto. The rider with the best combined score wins.

In supercross and endurocross races, riders try to finish well in **qualifying races**. The top riders make it to the main event. The first finisher in this race wins!

INNOVATOR OF THE SPORT

name: **Ricky Carmichael**
birthdate: **November 27, 1979**
hometown: **Tallahassee, Florida**
innovations: **Completed two perfect motocross racing seasons in 2002 and in 2004**

GLOSSARY

challenging—difficult and requires a lot of work

classes—different groups of races organized by engine size

jersey—a shirt with padding to protect the rider

lapped—behind the leader by at least one complete lap

obstacles—bumps and jumps that challenge motocross riders

organized—planned ahead of time

qualifying races—early races in a competition; the top riders from the qualifying races make it to the main event.

steep—almost straight up and down

TO LEARN MORE

AT THE LIBRARY

Adamson, Thomas K. *Motocross Freestyle*. Minneapolis, Minn.: Bellwether Media, 2016.

Mara, Wil. *Extreme Motocross*. New York, N.Y.: Marshall Cavendish, 2013.

Polydoros, Lori. *Motocross Greats*. Mankato, Minn.: Capstone Press, 2012.

ON THE WEB

Learning more about motocross racing is as easy as 1, 2, 3.

1. Go to www.factsurfer.com.

2. Enter "motocross racing" into the search box.

3. Click the "Surf" button and you will see a list of related web sites.

With factsurfer.com, finding more information is just a click away.

INDEX

Blazusiak, Taddy, 4, 7

Carmichael, Ricky, 21

classes, 18

enduro, 10, 11

endurocross, 4, 7, 10, 11, 20

Europe, 12

gear, 16-17

hillclimbs, 10, 11

innovator, 21

jumps, 4, 8, 12

Los Angeles, California, 15

main event, 20

motorcycles, 7, 8, 12, 13

motos, 11, 18, 19

obstacles, 10

qualifying races, 20

scoring, 19

scrambles, 11, 13

speed, 4, 15

stadiums, 8, 10, 15

Superbowl of Motocross, 15

supercross, 8, 11, 15, 20

Tallahassee, Florida, 21

tracks, 8, 12

trails, 10, 12

trials, 11, 13

United States, 15

whoops, 8, 11

X Games, 4, 7

The images in this book are reproduced through the courtesy of: Juan Martinez, front cover; Ezra Shaw/ Getty Images, pp. 4-5, 6-7, 7; Imago/ Zuma Press, p. 8; Brian Ciancio/ Zuma Press, p. 9; PhotoStock10, pp. 10, 17; Lisi Niesner/ Reuters/ Corbis, p. 11; National Motor Museum/ Heritage Images/ Getty Images, pp. 12-13; Eric Schweikardt/ Sports Illustrated/ Getty Images, pp. 14-15; Zero Creatives/ Corbis, p. 16; sippakorn, p. 18; Frank Bienewald/ LightRocket/ Getty Images, p. 19; Del Mecum/ Cal Sport Media/ Newscom, p. 20; Reed Saxon/ AP/ Corbis, p. 21; Philipe Ancheta, p. 21 (bottom).